S0-AEG-976

A living symbol of freedom, wilderness, and power, a grizzly bear stands amid September tundra near Stony Hill. Alaska contains more than ninety-eight percent of the United States' population of grizzly bears (same species as brown bears), and more than seventy percent of the North American population. An estimated two hundred to three hundred grizzlies live in Denali National Park.

A midnight sunset glows off snow-streaked mountains above the Toklat River in late June. During this magical time of year—when the daylength lasts twenty hours—the sun sets around midnight and rises at about 4:00 A.M., and pale light lingers in the the sky through the night.

A summer solstice alpenglow warms the sky and a ridgeline above Thorofare Pass, near Eielson Visitor Center.
(Opposite) In mid-September, a sunset moon rises over Pioneer Ridge and the snowy north summit of Denali, 19,470' above sea level.

IN DENALI

A PHOTOGRAPHIC ESSAY OF
DENALI NATIONAL PARK & PRESERVE
ALASKA

TEXT AND PHOTOGRAPHS BY
KIM HEACOX

Copyright © 1992 Kim Heacox
All rights reserved.

Portions of "The Mountains" previously appeared in *Travel and Leisure* magazine,
and "The Riddle" in *National Parks* magazine, and are reprinted herein with
permission from American Express Publishing and the National Parks
and Conservation Association, respectively.

For their assistance, encouragement and/or inspiration, a sincere thanks to:
Edward Abbey, Wendell Berry, Robert M. Butterfield, Lewis Carroll, Steve Carwile,
Douglas H. Chadwick, Sue E. Dodge, Robert Dunn, Loren Eiseley, Ralph Waldo
Emerson, Melanie Heacox, Fred Hirschmann, Ken Kehrer, Aldo Leopold, Henry
Wadsworth Longfellow, Adolf Murie, Olaus Murie, Galen Rowell, John Ruskin,
Karen Schlom, Charles Sheldon, Robert Louis Stevenson, Henry David Thoreau,
and Jonathan Waterman.

Companion Press
Santa Barbara, California
Jane Freeburg, Publisher

Designed by Linda Trujillo

Printed and bound in Hong Kong
by Dai Nippon Printing Co., Ltd.

ISBN 0-944197-18-3 (paperback)
ISBN 0-944197-19-1 (clothbound)

*(Above) Spokes of sunlight spill through the
rocky spires of the Tokosha Mountains along
the south flank of the Alaska Range.
(Opposite) A pasque flower, sign of spring
in Denali, nods in sunlight after having been
anointed in a rain storm.*

9 8 7 6 5 4 3 2

For Melanie

The blue blossoms of dwarf forget-me-not, together with yellow lichen, brighten a talus slope at 4,000 feet near the summit of Igloo Mountain. Several species of wildflowers—poppies, spring beauties, saxifrages and others—grow at higher elevations in the park, hugging the earth and surviving in micro-climates of relatively windless air between rock crevices. Field botanists have found purple mountain saxifrage flowering in the park as high as 7,000 feet on the north side of the Alaska Range.

Amid a clearing storm and a summer sunset, a double rainbow arcs over Healy Ridge. In the foreground, thousands of flowering mountain avens appear like constellations across the tundra.

A male willow ptarmigan, the state bird of Alaska, perches alertly in a
willow. One of only a few bird species that live year-round in Denali, the
ptarmigan molts from white in winter to brown in summer—the better to
avoid detection by the red foxes, golden eagles, and gyrfalcons that hunt it.

Preface

*I*n Denali. The view is familiar, yet I do not take it for granted. My tent door opens onto a Pleistocene land shaped by ice and water, largely unchanged over the past ten thousand years. Largely wilderness. Glaciers, mountains, rivers, forests, tundra; a landscape rich with places that have never felt the tread of human feet, and it thrills me not because I could break first ground, but because such ground remains unbroken.

I shake the frost off my sleeping bag and get up. It is mid-September, crystal clear and cold. The air cuts with winter's edge. Sunrise paints the Alaska Range in soft pastels, with a blush of pink on the highest peak, the mountain the Athabascans called *Denali*, The High One—best known today as McKinley, in honor of a president who had neither a passion for mountains nor an interest in Alaska.

Bound from nesting grounds in the Yukon-Kuskokwim River deltas, or perhaps from farther north in Arctic Alaska, sandhill cranes migrate through Denali for winter feeding grounds as far south as New Mexico and the gulf coast of Texas.

This book respectfully refers to the mountain, and the park, by their native and more proper name: Denali. The words and images that follow are not an end in themselves, but a beginning. An invitation. There are no photographs of roadside wolves, or northern red-backed voles, or purple mountain saxifrages or Paleozoic phyllites. Instead, I offer glimpses that attempt to convey the priceless value of wilderness in general, and Denali National Park and Preserve in particular.

Photography, by definition, is "writing with light," and the light in Denali can be exquisite. Yet some of my best times here have been without my camera, hiking free, climbing high. The important thing is to get off the bus; get out here, drink deeply of the still sweet air. And for at least a moment, put away the gadgets and let the wonder and mystery wash over you like summer rain.

And ask yourself, what photograph is more important than the welfare of the animal being photographed? What career, what business, what industry or development is more important than the wilderness integrity of a national park? Industry and development are not monsters pounding at Alaska's door, they're termites chewing away at the foundation, and Denali needs more development like Scrooge needs more shillings.

As long as we equate economic prosperity with growth, and growth requires the consumption of land, Denali will be threatened. "The perception of beauty is a moral test," wrote Henry David Thoreau nearly 150 years ago. Now, on the 75th anniversary of this great national park, we test our morality and hold in our hands one of the most precious yet rapidly disappearing gifts the earth can give: wilderness.

I hear music overhead, a fluting rhapsody in the sky. Sandhill cranes are flying, celebrating. I break camp, hoist my pack and hike across the autumn tundra, counting my blessings in Denali.

Kim Heacox
Denali National Park
Autumn, 1991

In the Kantishna Hills, a tundra palette is composed of the blue blossoms of harebells surrounded by red dwarf cranberries, dark crowberries, white lichens and Labrador tea (with the needle-like leaves, lower-left corner).

The braided Savage River flows north out of the Alaska Range and over open tundra where mew gulls and harlequin ducks often gather during the summer breeding season. Larger wildlife, such as caribou, wolves and foxes, use rivers in the mountains of Denali as migration and hunting corridors.

The River

Shallow at its edges, deep in the middle; a tireless agent of erosion and deposition, it runs turbid and tumbling toward the sea, as it has for ten thousand years and more. Here a riffle forms, there an eddy, elsewhere rapids rise and fall like a dragon's back, throwing droplets through the air.

I remove my boots. Am I really going to cross this river? I remove my socks. Of course I am. I roll up my pant legs. Should I reconsider this? I put on an old pair of tennis shoes brought along for crossing rivers. No, there's really nothing to reconsider. I tie my boots to my pack. Perhaps I should wait until morning. Nonsense, it's only a river. I hoist my pack onto my back and look for a place to cross.

Like most rivers in Denali, this one runs in channels that diverge, converge and diverge again, braiding across great beds of gravel, sand, cobbles, and rocks. All kinds of rocks: granite, gabbro and gneiss; limestone, sandstone and schist; chert, argillite and tuff; a veritable palette of earthtones and tectonics, the handiwork of aeons forged from the geologically complex Alaska Range, excavated by glaciers and moved and smoothed by the river.

The northbound Toklat River flows out of the Alaska Range past Divide Mountain during a midnight sunset in June. Its waters will join the Kantishna River, which will flow into the Tanana River, then the mighty Yukon and eventually the Bering Sea.

Longfellow once wrote about eyes: "Those only are beautiful which, like the planets, have a steady, lambent light . . . ." And so it is with this cross fox—a dark phase of a red fox—ever watchful next to the Toklat River. An omnivore, the fox eats muskrats, squirrels, birds, eggs, insects, vegetation, carrion, and—its preferred food—voles. An opportunist, it might den in enlarged marmot burrows, or abandoned wolf dens, and it frequently travels the road in Denali while hunting.

I walk on, looking for a spot where the channels are numerous and the water shallow. Unlike the river, the channels themselves are temporary, sooner or later—this year, next year, ten or one hundred years from now—a dam of sediment or ice will form, the water will flood around it, and a new channel will be born.

This spot looks good. I plunge in. Five steps later I'm flooded to my knees, my legs are half-numb and I'm less than one-third the way across the first channel. The current is strong and hypnotizing. My footing shifts; I stumble and nearly fall. Every passing second I stand in mid-current, the odds stack against me. Should I continue? Yes, I think.

I look up to catch my bearings, and to my surprise I am not alone. Staring at me from the opposite side of the farthest channel is a red fox.

Most foxes I have seen are on the move, hunting, heading out, heading home, often with a ptarmigan or arctic ground squirrel in its jaws, but this one sits on its haunches and stares at me with amber, cat-like eyes. My legs go completely numb, and it occurs to me that I must look as peculiar to the fox, standing thigh-deep in the river, as the fox looks to me, sitting stone-still on the bank.

Certainly no fox would cross this river, not here at this time of year. Farther upstream, maybe. In winter when things are frozen, probably. But here and now, in this turbid, roaring, subarctic, glacial meltwater river? Never. Foxes know their limitations; they have their boundaries. They survive.

I turn around. The cold is more than uncomfortable; it is painful. Five steps from the bank and I'm biting my lip. Rocks tumble against my ankles. Four steps; my head is pounding. Three steps; the river goes shallow. Two steps. One. I stumble ashore and fall on the bank, gasping. My legs are red, my ankles bruised.

Pain, joy, water, rock, sun, wind; I lie next to the river and catch my breath. Sitting up, I look for the fox, but it has gone as quietly as it came; a hunter fleet-of-foot. I, too, must go. So listening to the river, learning from the fox, and feeling alive in a way only the wilderness can impart, I hoist my pack and turn upstream toward the mountains.

A band of Dall sheep rams (males) rests on a mountain slope near the east end of the park in late September. In the background, newly-fallen snow blankets the Alaska Range near the headwaters of the Sanctuary River.

The Mountains

*I*t takes four hours of steady uphill hiking to reach the top of the ridge. Not many people go there, but I do at least once a year, mostly to see Dall sheep, the only species of wild white sheep in the world. A band of about thirty live up there, mostly rams with sweeping horns and penetrating golden-brown eyes. The ewes have shorter horns and keep a close watch over their lambs that gambol over the tundra on legs as light as wings.

Storms that send me scurrying for cover hardly faze them. They graze on green, summer slopes, always within close reach of rocky cliffs for protection from wolves. Every so often a golden eagle will dive on them, hitting a lamb hard enough to kill it, or knocking an adult off a rocky ledge where it falls to its death. Survival is a daily chore.

Whenever I think I know all about them, they do something new; a twitch, a posture, a nuzzle, a challenge. Once I witnessed a ram walk a ledge that narrowed until there was no

A pair of adolescent Dall sheep rams, having approached the photographer as he sat still, are warmed by an amber sunset on a mountain ridge.

room to turn around. Undaunted, he simply planted his front hooves and rotated his hind legs up the rocky wall behind him, over his head until he faced the opposite direction and walked back to find another route.

Feeling smug, I like to think these sheep have grown comfortable with me. Several times they have bedded down right outside my tent, once so close that a ram blocked the entrance and I couldn't get out. I quietly zipped open the door and he was ten feet away, staring at me in a transcendental moment, species to species.

I could no more shoot one than I could strangle a child. Yes, if I were starving it would be different. And yes, hunting is part of our human ancestry, like cave dwelling. But since the Age of Enlightenment and its contemporary counterpart—the Age of Environmentalism—the game has ended, the sport has soured. And speciesism, like racism and sexism, has been labeled a particularly human blend of arrogance and ignorance. Perhaps only when we stop shooting wild animals will we stop shooting each other. "A man is rich in proportion to the number of things he can afford to let alone," wrote Henry David Thoreau. Do wild landscapes tell us anything of true wealth?

Denali National Park is a Walden Pond; a place to practice humility and respect.

In Autumn the tundra turns from green to gold to red. The snow falls. The last time I see the sheep, the rams are charging and butting heads in the autumn air, and the lambs are close to their mothers' sides.

Winter sets down as cold as steel, and I retreat to my home just a few miles from the park entrance, thinking about the sheep in the darkness of winter at forty below, day after day, month after month. They are up on that mountain, huddled together, watching for wolves, scraping for food, surviving. A few die each year from predation, starvation, rock slides, and avalanches. But the band survives. And climbing back up there and seeing them the next spring is, for me, a sight filled with miracle and promise.

In the warmth and tranquility of a late August sunset, a solitary hiker is framed by Reflection Pond and 11,880-foot Mt. Brooks, twenty-two miles distant in the Alaska Range.

A September sunset warms the tundra near the Savage River. At roughly 63 degrees north latitude, Denali National Park and Preserve is more than twice as close to the North Pole as it is to the Equator, making for long, cold winters and short, cool summers.

The Promise

She came from Cincinnati and was fond of telling people that Ohio was once so wild a squirrel could cross the entire state by jumping from tree to tree without ever touching the ground. She was a grandmother who loved her children and grandchildren, and cherished her time with them every day, especially summer days with long evenings and family dinners on the back porch.

But as she had aged and lost her youth, Ohio had lost its wildness. For reasons even she could not explain, it left her feeling impoverished. Something inside of her was missing. Ohio was gone, like Indiana, Illinois, Michigan, Wisconsin, Iowa, and on and on and on. Wild America had been plowed, fenced, dammed, and clearcut, and the grandmother had lost touch with the earth, with places untrammeled, unruly, uncultivated, uncivilized. The Saturday mall made her sad. Nature was not a potted plant in the window or a squirrel in the park; it was bears and wolves and freedom in immense, wild ecosystems. So she made herself a promise: Go to Alaska.

Swarmed by mosquitoes and backlit by sunset, a bull caribou moves through the tundra near Wonder Lake. Caribou will frequently stampede to a wind-blown ridge or cool snowfield in search of relief from biting insects.

Some of her family supported her, but most considered her crazy, senile. She paid thousands of dollars, came alone, and loved it. Especially Denali.

"Bear," she yelled as the bus rumbled along the road. The driver stopped. "Behind those bushes by that creek," she said. The other passengers shifted in their seats and pulled out cameras, video-recorders, and binoculars. Suddenly a Toklat grizzly, a race of blond bear common in Denali, moved into view and over the tundra with a wild viscosity preserved from the Pleistocene—the Ice Age—stopping here to eat berries, there to dig for roots. It approached the bus with its fur haloed in the light of the morning sun.

The grandmother was thrilled. But unlike most everyone else on the bus, she had no camera or video-recorder. She didn't want them. Better to see the magnificent bear unobstructed by plastic and glass, uncluttered by f-stops and shutter speeds. Better to have a vision quest, she thought to herself; to preserve the moment on the sensitive emulsion of her mind.

She opened the window. The bear moved closer. The driver asked everyone to be quiet. The bear climbed the bank, emerged on the road and walked past the bus, only a few feet from the grandmother. She held her breath and didn't move.

"What did you do then?" asked her twelve-year-old grandson a week later back in Ohio.

The grandmother smiled. "I prayed that someday you will go to Alaska and see the same thing," she told him. "That you will see wild bears on the tundra, eagles on the cliffs, and wildflowers at your feet. That you will take a discovery hike with a ranger and learn about wilderness."

"Oh," her grandson said.

"Listen," she told him as she took his hand. "You know I love you, and I've never asked you for anything, but I am now. Protect the wild bear and the wilderness where it lives, and ask your children to do the same. Because if we lose the wilderness and the bear, a spirit will die, and a part of each of us will die with it."

Scott Peak (8,828') wears a mantle of fresh snow above the Thorofare River in mid-September. Soon the entire scene will be whitened by snow, the river will freeze and rangers with sled dog teams will patrol through here en route to and from park headquarters and the Wonder Lake Ranger Station.

Testimony to the Ice Age, a lichen-covered rock sits on the tundra above Wonder Lake, probably deposited by a glacier from the Alaska Range thirty miles distant. The same glacier may have carved a nearby depression that later filled with water—280 feet deep—to become Wonder Lake.

The Riddle

 *A*mong the riddles of the ancient Chinese is one about a man who discovers the most beautiful place in the world. The riddle is a conundrum: a puzzle without a solution, because the man shares his discovery, and people flock there in such great numbers that the place is changed forever, and is beautiful no more.

It is the pioneer's paradox, the process of people destroying, or at least eroding, the very thing they love, often the natural environment, and it exists not only in ancient China but throughout the entire modern world. Though national parks should be exempt from this, they are not.

And Denali? Will the same mistakes made elsewhere be made here? Or will people learn that to truly save a place they must close doors in front of them, rather than behind them? Hopefully, Alaska will escape the Manifest Destiny mentality that fenced, paved, and tamed the lower forty-eight states, and we who can alter any landscape in the world will have the wisdom to leave this one alone.

From near Wonder Lake, two hikers enjoy a clear view of the north summit of Denali (19,470') and the north-facing Wickersham Wall, twenty-seven miles distant and rising without preamble more than fourteen thousand feet—one of the greatest unbroken vertical rises in the world.

It is vital, of course, that people come here; that lives are touched and inspired, that wilderness values are affirmed and anxieties washed away. Yet it is equally vital, in a world of greed, and conundrums, that visitors not be herded into mediocrity, that the park experience—and the park itself—not be impaired in any way, or even jeopardized.

At six million acres, Denali National Park and Preserve is about the same size as Massachusetts, nearly three times the size of Yellowstone. Running through it are icy mountains that break their backs in the Alaska Range, their summits reaching to 14,000 feet, 17,000 feet, and finally to 20,320-foot Mt. McKinley, more properly called *Denali*—the native name meaning The High One—the highest mountain in North America.

From the mountains, the land sweeps to every horizon in striking patterns of tundra and spruce forest, kettle ponds and braided rivers, wildflowers and willow thickets. More than 600 species of trees, shrubs, and herbs live here, some growing profusely in protected valleys, others hugging windswept ridges in button, mat, and rosette shapes.

Every summer, from eastern Siberia, the Pacific, Latin and North America, birds arrive to raise their young. Shorebirds nest on the tundra, raptors on the cliffs; more than 150 species occur here. But Denali's most sought-after residents are the large mammals: grizzlies, wolves, caribou, moose, Dall sheep, red foxes, lynx, and others—thirty-seven species of mammals in all. Nothing stimulates the heart more than the sudden appearance of a bear, a wolf, or a caribou moving over the land with wild, ancient poetry. Like the birds and plants, they fit into the landscape as an integral part of a greater whole, manifesting laws of survival and diversity, embodying what has been called "the greatest subarctic sanctuary in the world."

This, then, is what Charles Sheldon found when he came to Interior Alaska in the summer of 1906. A member of the influential Boone & Crockett Club, he was cut from the same conservation cloth as Teddy Roosevelt. A hunter, yes, but more than that a competent and caring naturalist who traveled widely throughout Denali by foot, snowshoe, and sled dog team.

Looking north, a 3:00 A.M. sunrise reddens the channels of the Toklat River in mid-June. Near here, in the winter of 1907–08, conservationist Charles Sheldon built a cabin (now in ruins) and developed his ideas and strategies for the creation of Denali National Park.

Camped on a moraine above the Peters Glacier in January, 1908, with the land and silence all to himself, Sheldon wrote, "When Denali Park shall be made easy of access with accommodations and facilities for travel . . . . it is not difficult to anticipate the enjoyment and inspiration visitors will receive."

Many decades later, Sheldon's prediction has come true. Enjoyment and inspiration are commonplace among visitors to Denali. But will it remain that way?

In 1971, the year before the highway was completed between Anchorage and Fairbanks—connecting Denali to Alaska's two largest cities—annual park visitation was 30,000. Twenty years later 600,000 visitors came. A single dirt road, built in the 1920s and '30s, winds ninety miles through the park, cutting into mountainsides, crossing rivers, traversing open expanses of tundra and spruce forest. Dozens of buses travel that road every day of summer, each carrying about forty people who admire the scenery and watch for wildlife.

The bus system works on two premises: by reducing private vehicle traffic along the road it minimizes the risk of accidents, and maximizes the opportunities to view wildlife that otherwise might be displaced by more traffic.

But to those addicted to power and money, Denali is not being fully "utilized." Build another hotel, they say. Add more rooms. Add more buses, another road, a railroad, a monorail, a tramway. Anydamnthing. As for environmental impact, don't worry. Rangers scrutinize and scientists hypothesize, but MONEY TALKS!

Here, then, is a way of thinking that believes Denali National Park should be accessible to as many people as possible; that tourism, like cattle-ranching, is a volume-driven meat market; that scenery, more than anything else, is a commodity.

If the finest hotels can have "no vacancy," if the greatest concert halls can have limited seating, then why not our national parks? The theater is full; you are invited to the next performance. "It is the expansion of transport without a corresponding growth of perception that threatens us with qualitative bankruptcy of the recreational process," wrote Aldo Leopold in *A Sand County Almanac.* "Recreational development is a job not of building roads into lovely country, but of building receptivity into the still unlovely human mind."

In a sweeping, grandiose state where the words "Last Frontier" carry the old, false assumptions of limitless resources and opportunities; where a political system embraces economic growth as though it were a religion, where the National Park Service must answer to that same political system—the best government money can buy, composed of men and women whose idea of a land ethic is as thin as a dollar bill—and where industrial tourism advances slowly and inexorably, like the tide; then if this is the way it is, and shall be, Denali is doomed. Not to a disaster, but to a slow, insidious strangulation of its wilderness integrity.

Something has to change. Lines must be drawn and defended. For only then will Denali and other national parks remain pristine, and will landscapes beat to the rhythms of something more ancient than us all. Here, people will say, is a piece of the earth as it once was, and should forever remain: absolutely wild.

A clearing summer storm veils Healy Ridge near the park's eastern boundary.

A shuttle bus carries visitors over Polychrome Pass at 3,700 feet, near mile 46 on the park road. The rocks in the talus slope below, through which the road is cut and the bus is traveling, belong to the upper half of the Cantwell Formation; they are volcanic—mostly rhyolite, andesite and basalt—formed from magma approximately sixty million years ago. Today, the cliffs above them (from near where this photograph was taken) offer excellent nesting sites for gyrfalcons and golden eagles. In years of abundant prey, more than fifty pairs of golden eagles have been found nesting in the park.

*Among the lucky few who have a clear view of Denali—at 20,320 feet,
North America's highest mountain—are these visitors enjoying a lunch
break at the Stony Hill Overlook, 36 miles east of the mountain.*

Dall sheep rams gather on a ridge in rich September light. Unlike moose and caribou (members of the deer family that grow new sets of antlers every year) Dall sheep horns are retained for life. As the sheep ages, the horns enlarge and lengthen into a circle when seen from the side—each year adds another growth ring. Ram horns reach half a circle in about 2–3 years, three-quarters of a circle in 4–5 years, and "full curl" in 7–11 years.

"The lambs play a great deal, romping with speed and agility," wrote naturalist/biologist Adolf Murie about Dall sheep lambs in Denali National Park. Born in late May and early June, the lambs stay close to their mothers until they are weaned in early October.

A bull caribou stands silhouetted on a ridge near Mt. Galen. For reasons not entirely understood, population cycles seem to be the rule, rather than the exception, among Alaska's barren ground caribou. The Denali herd, which numbered an estimated thirty thousand in the 1940s, crashed to two thousand in the 1980s, and now appears to be increasing again.

Antlers blood-red from the recently-shed velvet that nourished them, a bull caribou pauses amid rust-colored dwarf birch in the Kantishna Hills. In winter, after the autumn rut (mating), he will "drop" his antlers and begin growing a new set the following spring. Caribou are the only member of the deer family to grow antlers on both sexes, though the females' are much smaller. Caribou migrate between summer calving grounds and winter feeding grounds. To help protect the Denali herd year-round, 1.9-million acre Mt. McKinley National Park (created in 1917) was enlarged in 1980 to 6.0-million acre Denali National Park and Preserve.

"Where our last frontiers remain good enough for the grizzly," wrote Douglas H. Chadwick in National Geographic *magazine, "they will be good enough for all the other wild things that need homes and space and a little respect. And they will be good enough, big enough, wild enough, free enough for us."*

A bull moose is silhouetted in Wonder Lake as a September sunrise paints Denali, thirty miles away, in pastel morning light. By the end of October the moose will have finished rut (mating), and by the end of January dropped its antlers, a cycle repeated each year. New antlers will begin to grow in the spring.

"For my part," wrote Robert Louis Stevenson in 1879, "I travel not to go anywhere, but to go. I travel for travel's sake. The great affair is to move." And what better way to move through Interior Alaska than by train, bound to and from Denali between Fairbanks and Anchorage. Built from 1915 to 1923 (from Seward to Fairbanks) the Alaska Railroad arrives in the park every day of summer, carrying visitors who often enjoy the journey as much as the destination.

A summer solstice sunset warms the spruce-covered slopes and mountain peaks above the Nenana River, which forms part of the eastern boundary of Denali National Park.

"Everybody should go down the river," wrote wilderness advocate Edward Abbey, "What river? Well, some river. Some kind of river. Huck Finn said that, and if he didn't, he should have. If he didn't, I will." These rafters are about to enter the Nenana River Gorge, a Precambrian chasm carved over milllions of years by a river that predated the rising of the mountains, and thus held its course as the land lifted around it.

Hang On! Rafters plunge wide-eyed and soaking wet through the Nenana River's Razorback Rapids. Thousands of tourists ride down the Nenana every summer through both wild and calm waters.

*O*n the high road to adventure, a west-bound shuttle bus near Thorofare Pass (el. 3,900') is dwarfed by Denali, thirty-five miles away and more than 16,000 feet higher. The twin summits are two miles apart and separated by the Harper Glacier. The south Peak (on the left) is the highest point in North America and was first climbed in June of 1913 by Walter Harper, Robert Tatum, Harry Karstens (who in 1921 became the first superintendent of Denali) and expedition leader Hudson Stuck, Episcopal Archdeacon of the Yukon, who earlier had remarked "I would rather climb that mountain than discover the richest gold mine in Alaska." The North Peak (on the right, 19,470') was first climbed in April of 1910 by the Sourdough Expedition—four miners who had never climbed a mountain before. Fortified with doughnuts and hot chocolate, and using a fast-and-light climbing style that would not be popularized by alpinists for another seventy years, three of the Sourdoughs (Billy Taylor, Pete Anderson and Charles McGonagall) made a one-day-dash for the peak from their 12,000-foot base camp on the Muldrow Glacier. Taylor and Anderson made it, but didn't stay long: the summit temperature was thirty degrees below zero. They planted a fourteen-foot spruce pole in some rocks at about 19,000' and returned to disbelieving audiences in Kantishna and Fairbanks. Three years later the Sourdough story was vindicated when the Stuck Party, victorious atop the South Peak, focused their binoculars on the North Peak and saw the spruce pole still standing.

*B*ruin blockade! A grizzly bear meets a shuttle bus on the park road near Stony Hill Overlook. Though thrilling for the people on board, this encounter is a disturbance for the bear (which is standing and studying the bus probably more out of curiosity than aggression). Wildlife should be observed without their behavior being altered, for Denali is not a circus, a zoo or a garden, and should never be treated even remotely as such. "All the plants and animals enjoy a natural and normal life without human restrictions," wrote biologist Adolf Murie about Denali. "Our task is to perpetuate this freedom and purity of nature, this ebb and flow of life— first, by insuring ample park boundaries so that the region is large enough to maintain the natural relationships, and secondly, to hold man's intrusions to a minimum."

The Long and Winding Road

The journey by road through Denali National Park is widely regarded as one of the most scenic in Alaska. The following are mileages and elevations along the way:

0.0 MILE/1,590 FEET *The road west into the park begins at mile 237.3 on the George Parks Highway between Anchorage and Fairbanks.*

0.7 MILE/1,660 FEET *Visitor Access Center*

1.5 MILE/1,730 FEET *Railroad station & park hotel*

3.4 MILE/2,055 FEET *Park headquarters & dog kennels (most of the buildings were built in the 1930s)*

12.8 MILE/2,780 FEET *Savage River Campground. Two miles farther, the pavement ends at the Savage River Bridge.*

22.5 MILE/2,470 FEET *Sanctuary River*

29.1 MILE/2,580 FEET *Teklanika Campground*

34.1 MILE/2,940 FEET *Igloo Campground*

39.1 MILE/3,900 FEET *Sable Pass*

43.4 MILE/3,040 FEET *East Fork of the Toklat River*

45.9 MILE/3,700 FEET *Polychrome Pass*

53.1 MILE/3,090 FEET *Toklat River*

58.3 MILE/3,980 FEET *Highway Pass, the road's highest point.*

62.0 MILE/3,900 FEET *Stony Hill Overlook*

64.5 MILE/3,950 FEET *Thorofare Pass*

66.0 MILE/3,730 FEET *Eielson Visitor Center*

84.6 MILE/2,290 FEET *Road junction. Low road leads to Wonder Lake Campground and the end of the shuttle bus line; high road leads to Wonder Lake Ranger Station and the settlement of Kantishna.*

86.1 MILE/2,090 FEET *Wonder Lake Campground*

86.7 MILE/2,110 FEET *Wonder Lake Ranger Station. From here the road continues north, ending at Kantishna airstrip, mile 91.5.*

"It rose like an unearthly castle of opalescent glass," wrote Robert Dunn, a journalist and amateur mountaineer, after he and his party failed to reach the summit of Denali in 1903. "Something besides courage and determination is needed to climb a mountain like this. Forgive me if I call it intelligence." Not until 1913 would the highest mountain in North America be successfully climbed, not until 1947 would a woman reach the top, and not until 1951 would the safest and most popular route—the West Buttress—be pioneered.

It is a long, hard walk, not especially technical, yet always with an element of danger due to capricious weather, and the possibility of sudden onset of fatigue and high altitude sickness. In his book *High Alaska*, author/mountaineer Jonathan Waterman writes, "Because of Denali's height and position just south of the Arctic Circle, it is arguably the coldest mountain on earth." As many as one thousand climbers attempt Denali and its satellite peaks each year (usually from April to June), and roughly half reach the top. Over the years, this great, breathtaking, dangerous mountain has claimed the lives of more than fifty climbers, many of them experts; more than thirty remain buried up there somewhere in the ice and snow.

From Wonder Lake Campground, Denali—only twenty-seven miles away—rises to the roof of North America. "Mountains are the beginning and the end of all natural scenery," wrote John Ruskin a century and a half ago. With a vista like this, you can hardly challenge his point of view. Yet even cold, overcast days are rewarding here as well, with tundra patterns, bird songs, sweet berries, wildflowers and wildlife to enrich a sensitive heart.

"Alaska has for most of us a magic ring," wrote Adolph Murie in A Naturalist in Alaska, *as if thinking of this unnamed creek flowing from an unnamed mountain in Denali. "It is still a frontier, and chiefly a big wilderness . . . a land where the individual is not yet swamped by numbers." The challenge today— indeed, our obligation—is to keep it that way.*

The bleached remains of a dead spruce rise like supplicating arms amid red bearberry leaves above the Savage River Valley. In the distance is Healy Ridge, near the east entrance to the park.

"If there is magic in this world," wrote Loren Eiseley, *"it is contained in water."* And nothing compliments water more than light, such as this cinnabar midnight sunset along the Toklat River in June.

Silent, still and inconspicuous, a female Lapland longspur sits in her nest on the open tundra. Come fall, with her family hatched and fledged, she will migrate south to winter feeding grounds in the contiguous United States.

A red-necked grebe sits on its nest near the southern boundary of the park, while its mate stays close behind. Diving birds with lobed toes for strong swimming, grebes feed primarily on small fish and other aquatic and marine life. The red-necked is one of seven species of grebes that occur in North America. Come fall, this pair will probably fly to wintering areas along the coast of Alaska, British Columbia or the western United States.

A young grizzly bear, busily scratching his/her back on a picnic table, studies a shuttle bus as it drives past Stony Hill Overlook, at MILE 62.0 on the park road.

A grizzly bear looks up from eating in the September tundra near Wonder Lake. At this time of year grizzlies eat at a furious rate—a phenomenon called "hyperphagia," which in Greek literally means "excessive consumption." Scatalogical studies have determined that an adult grizzly in hyperphagia may eat upwards of 200,000 berries per day; blueberries, soapberries, cranberries, crowberries, all to add body fat that will sustain it during the long hibernation ahead.

Amid the reflection of golden autumn grasses, a beaver—the largest member of the rodent family—swims in a pond near Wonder Lake, busily preparing for winter. Once the pond freezes over, a beaver family will spend much of the winter warm and secure in their lodge.

Newly-fallen September snow mantles the shoulders of Panorama Mountain, above a nameless pond just outside the southeast boundary of the park.

Yellow cinquefoil, a member of the rose family, blossoms on a rocky bluff near Polychrome Pass, a preferred habitat of Dall sheep, hoary marmots, golden eagles and gyrfalcons. Below stretches a braided river on the Plains of Murie; beyond the Alaska Range.

A hoary marmot keeps watch from atop a favorite rock. Should an intruder approach, the marmot will sound the alarm with a loud whistle, and usually dash into a burrow. A highly social animal, the marmot lives with its family that together with other family burrows nearby forms a colony.

From MILE *118 on the George Parks Highway, near the settlements of Trapper Creek and Talkeetna, Denali rises approximately 55 miles to the north-northwest. "Stupendous," wrote Captain George Vancouver when he sighted the mountain from Cook Inlet, far to the south, in 1794.*

The warm, variegated tones of sunset wash over spruce-covered slopes near the park entrance. Because Denali National Park and Preserve is located in the subarctic, between 62 and 64 degrees north latitude, treeline here averages only 2,500 to 3,000 feet in elevation.

The large, palmate leaves of devil's club spread beneath a forest of birch and spruce along the Chulitna River, about thirty miles south of Denali National Park, next to the southern boundary of Denali State Park. Here the subarctic climate of Interior Alaska begins to surrender to the temperate climate of southcentral Alaska.

Yellow marsh saxifrage, also called bog saxifrage, grows along a quiet stream that runs through wet tundra below the Eielson Bluffs. As many as seventeen species of saxifrage occur in Denali, growing in such diverse habitats as gravel bars, ridge tops, talus slopes, forest floors, dry tundra and wet tundra. Good field botanists recognize saxifrage blossoms as having five sepals, five petals, ten stamens and a deep (sometimes conical) ovary.

A red squirrel busily scampers through a spruce tree doing what it does best: cutting and collecting cones for summer and winter storage. Blind, hairless, and weighing only a quarter of an ounce at birth, the red squirrel quickly matures into an agile, furry climber, jumping from branch to branch and tree to tree, chattering at trespassers and vigorously defending its territory, which averages one-half to one acre. Its preferred food is seeds (from cones), berries, buds, fungi and an occasional insect or bird egg. Chief predators are hawks, owls and the marten, a relative of the mink. Unlike the arctic ground squirrel (opposite) the red squirrel does not hibernate in winter.

Conspicuous resident of the open tundra, an arctic ground squirrel surveys its domain and feeds on grasses, flowering plants, berries, roots, mosses and lichens while keeping a watchful eye for predators. Called the "bread and butter" of the Denali tundra, this abundant rodent provides a significant portion of the meat diet of red foxes, gyrfalcons, golden eagles, wolves and grizzly bears. Under pursuit, a ground squirrel will dash down its burrow, a safe escape most of the time. A determined grizzly, however, will excavate a huge pit in the tundra to get the squirrel. Sometimes the bear is successful, other times the squirrel emerges from a distant, connected burrow and watches, from behind, as the great bear digs in futility.

"The earth laughs in flowers," wrote Ralph Waldo Emerson. In Denali, that laughter has many dialects—from alpine azalea (opposite page, upper left), a member of the heath family, growing among lichen-covered rocks; to the cream-colored blossoms of Lapland diapensia (upper right); to lingonberry (lower left) also known as low-bush cranberry, blooming in May amid fallen spruce cones; to shrubby cinquefoil (lower right), also known as tundra rose, growing next to Paleozoic schist in Savage River Canyon. On this page grows a stalk of bluebells, a member of the borage family, heavy with rain from a recent storm. Late June is the peak time for wildflowers in Denali, for then serious field botanists can find more than one hundred flowering species in a day, hiking from habitat to habitat, enjoying the fresh air, the freedom, and the poetry of blossoms at their feet.

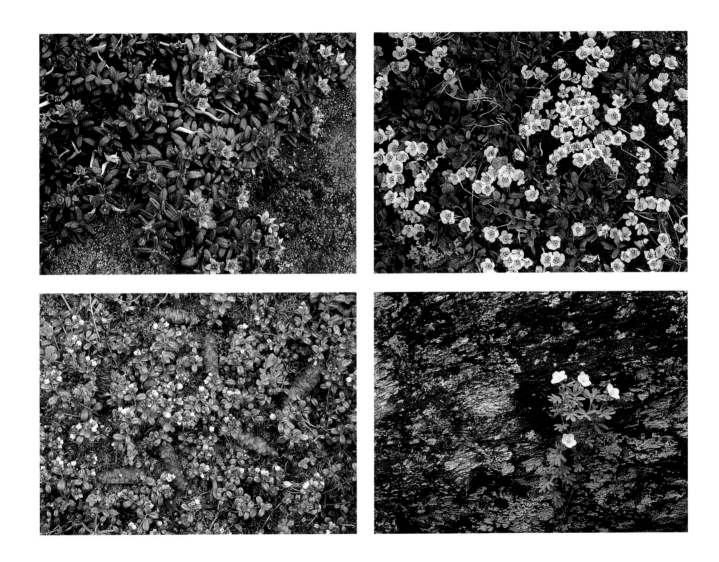

Denali National Park receives half its annual precipitation in June, July and August. It can rain for days straight, weeks, in fact; but when clouds part and the sun smiles, rainbows spread their wings, like this one over the Toklat River in July.

Tall fireweed, a perennial sign of summer, is complimented by a rainbow at 10:30 P.M. in July, on the north side of Mt. Healy, near the east entrance to the park. As the weeks go by, the lowest fireweed blossoms open first, and those on top last. When the final blossom falls from the very top, summer is said to be over.

Kim Heacox sets the timer on his camera and takes a self-portrait while cross-country skiing on the north side of the Alaska Range. The time is 6:00 P.M., early April; the temperature 20° F, the wind calm, the skiing perfect. In six weeks most of the snow will be gone and the first wildflowers will be out. And very soon, if not already, grizzly bears will be emerging from their winter dens.

"Now, in retrospect," wrote biologist/artist Olaus Murie in Journeys to the Far North, "I want to be back again with a loaded sled creaking its way over rough ice and running smoothly and quietly over level places, with a good team of dogs trotting steadily in front, muzzles low, tails waving high—and the snow stretching away until broken by the high line of woods where we might camp for the night." Dog sledding has been a winter way of life in Denali since the 1920s, when rangers began using teams of huskies on winter patrols, as they still do today.

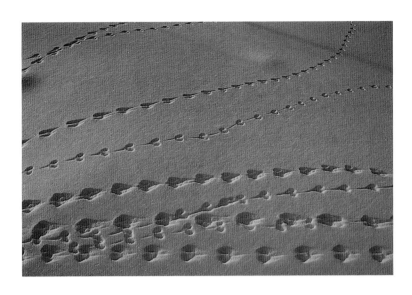

 Of the approximately 155 species of birds that spend their summers in Denali, or pass through, fewer than two dozen (sixteen percent) stay for the winter. One is the white-tailed ptarmigan, pictured opposite. Others include willow ptarmigan, rock ptarmigan, raven, black-billed magpie, boreal chickadee, gray jay, boreal owl, northern hawk owl, and gyrfalcon. Though average winter temperatures in Denali hover around zero degrees Fahrenheit, they regularly drop to twenty below. When the mercury sinks to fifty below (which usually happens at least once each winter) park employees remain at home. By December most rivers freeze over, snow blankets the land, and animals leave their tracks like signatures on winter's white parchment. While deep snow and solid ice can make grazing and browsing difficult for moose, caribou and Dall sheep, a blanket of snow is important for small subnivean ("beneath snow") mammals—such as voles and shrews—as it insulates them from the cold air above.

Mountaineers camp on a ridge above the Ruth Glacier, in the Don Sheldon Amphitheatre on Denali's southeast side. Many climbers begin ascents of Denali—which take an average of two to three weeks—landing by ski plane at about 7,100 feet on the nearby Kahiltna Glacier.

Skier Melanie Heacox passes a crevasse at 6,000 feet on the Ruth Glacier. Seventeen glaciers spill down the slopes of Denali, the largest of them on the south side. Snow falls here every month of the year, and the glaciers in some places are thousands of feet thick.

A cow (female) moose stands amid willows and winter snow in the east end of the park. In the early 1900s naturalist Charles Sheldon wrote that the "sight of a moose" stirred within him "the consciousness of the presence of a noble form of wildlife . . . evoking a sense of creatures of the long past." Though we might regard the moose as odd-looking—long legs, long snout, high shoulders—it is in fact well-adapted to life in the north. Long legs make for high stepping in deep snow, and hollow hairs insulate it to 70° below zero. Deep snow can take its toll, however, making browsing more difficult—a bull moose that weighs 1,500 pounds in September may lose 300 pounds by April. Deep snow conditions can force moose onto highways and railways where the walking is easier but the traffic dangerous.

Aside from the autumn rut (mating period) when courtship is in the air, Alaskan moose spend their time doing three things: feeding, resting, and moving to new feeding areas. Here a bull (male) moose rests amid July wildflowers near the headwaters of the Sanctuary River. A browser as well as grazer, the moose prefers willow, and in summer consumes an average of sixty pounds of leaves and twigs per day.

The icy, granite spires of the Great Gorge and Ruth Glacier rise in the distance behind a birch and spruce forest in September, along the Chulitna River and the southeast boundary of the park.

In the still air of an autumn evening, Reflection Pond captures the warmth of alpenglow on the north face of Denali and the Alaska Range. "Nature and books belong to those with the eyes that see them," wrote Ralph Waldo Emerson. Standing here, you believe him.

A primary feather from a mew gull rests on a tundra montage of autumn colors, composed of bearberry (large red leaves), blueberry (small leaves with water droplets below the feather), dwarf cranberry (also called lingonberry—small green leaves in upper right and center) and Labrador tea (needle-like leaves in lower right).

Alaska boykinia, also known as bear flower, grows along a stream near Thorofare Pass. A member of the saxifrage family, this flower typically grows next to streams and snowfields.

A snowshoe hare, also called varying hare, pauses in the forest underbrush before dashing for cover. Most active at dusk and dawn, hares feed on grasses, leaves, twigs and buds, and are fed upon by lynx, foxes and raptors. Their populations are highly cyclic, peaking every ten to eleven years with hundreds of hares per square mile, then crashing (for reasons not entirely understood) to only a few hares per square mile.

A male willow ptarmigan defends his territory from atop a spruce tree in mid-May. Ground nesters, ptarmigan females lay six to ten eggs and incubate them for three weeks. Hatching occurs in late June and early July. The chicks have partial flight capabilities in two weeks, and full flight capabilities in eight weeks.

The sun sets over the Teklanika River in a reddened, smoky sky caused by summer wildfires to the north. Although the smoke is a nuisance for visitors who expect clear vistas, wildfires are an important element in the ecology of Denali, contributing to nutrient cycling in the forests and tundra.

Snowshoeing into a March sunset at 9:00 P.M. offers beauty and silence along the old Stampede Trail, on the north side of the Alaska Range. At this time of year—a favorite among local residents—daylight increases by seven minutes a day, and the snowshoeing, dog sledding and cross-country skiing are exquisite.

A HUMAN HISTORY TIMETABLE

C. 1500 B.C. TO A.D. 1900
Native Alaskans hunted within Alaska's interior using temporary hunting camps, some of which were located within the current boundaries of Denali National Park & Preserve.

1896
William Dickey, a Princeton man, prospects for gold in Alaska. Although native people called the highest peak in the region *Denali*, "The High One," Dickey gives it the name "Mount McKinley" in honor of Ohio Congressman William McKinley, who had been nominated as a presidential candidate. The new name, published in the *New York Sun*, was later officially accepted by the U. S. Geological Survey for future maps.

1902
Alfred H. Brooks, a U.S.Geological Survey geologist, leads an expedition that reaches the foot of Denali (Mount McKinley), and makes the first useful map of the area. Estimating the mountain's elevation at 20,300', he makes the first known attempt to climb it, and reaches 7,500'.

1903
Territorial Judge James Wickersham attempts to climb Denali (Mount McKinley) with an expedition from Fairbanks. They ascend the Peters Glacier on the mountain's north side, reaching about 8,100 feet before finding the route impassable. Later, members of this expedition stake the first mining claims in the Kantishna Hills.

1904
Joseph Dalton and Joseph Quigley prospect in the basin of the Toklat River.

1905
Gold Rush! Stampeders arrive in the Kantishna Hills by the thousands. Eureka, a new boom town located in Kantishna, boasts 2,000 inhabitants.

1906
Charles Sheldon arrives for the summer to study Dall sheep and collect game specimens; he hires Harry Karstens as a guide. By fall, the gold boom is over—miners desert most areas in Kantishna.

1907–1908
Charles Sheldon and Harry Karstens spend the winter in the area mushing huskies and studying wildlife, and Sheldon develops the idea of Denali National Park. Gold is discovered in the Glen Creek area: the beginning of significant environmental destruction.

1910
Members of the Sourdough Expedition reach the summit of the north peak of Denali (Mount McKinley), and plant a fourteen-foot spruce flag pole with an American flag in a rock pile just below the summit. None of the members had climbed a mountain before; they fortified themselves with doughnuts and hot chocolate.

1913
Hudson Stuck, Harry Karstens, Walter Harper and Robert Tatum reach the summit of the south peak of Denali (Mount McKinley)—the first expedition to attain the highest point on the mountain and in North America.

1916
Maurice Morino homesteads and builds a roadhouse in the area. U. S. Congress holds hearings on the proposed Mount McKinley National Park.

1917
After a decade of lobbying efforts by Charles Sheldon and others, President Woodrow Wilson signs the bill establishing Mount McKinley National Park.

1921
Harry Karstens is hired as the new park's first superintendent, and stationed in Nenana.

1922
Park Headquarters is moved from Nenana to Riley Creek.

1923
Thirty-four visitors stay at the new Savage River Tourist Camp during the summer season. (Total park visitation is forty). The Alaska Railroad is completed between Seward and Fairbanks.

1924
Carl Ben Eielson, early Alaskan aviator, flies a WWI Jenny to Copper Mountain (now named Mount Eielson), landing on the Thorofare River gravel bar below the current location of Eielson Visitor Center. He brings a Fairbanks miner named Herning to place a mining claim. A forest fire burns near the park's entrance area.

1925
Thirteen miners remain in the Kanishna district recovering gold. Park Headquarters is moved from Riley Creek to its present location.

1926
Cabins are constructed at McKinley Bar (by Grant Pearson) and Sanctuary (by the Alaska Road Commission.) The park's sled dog kennels constructed.

1927
A stage coach road from the Savage River Tourist Camp to the head of the Savage River is completed; it remains in use until 1941. The Alaska Road Commission constructs Igloo cabin.

1928
Park visitation reaches 400–500 people, and forty miles of the park road are completed. Toklat and Copper Mountain (Mount Eielson) cabins are built, as well as rangers' quarters at park headquarters.

1929
Carl Ben Eielson dies in an airplane crash in Siberia. In 1930, Congress renames Copper Mountain Mount Eielson in his honor.

1932
The park's first seasonal naturalist is hired, and the park road reaches to Thorofare. Park boundaries are extended east to the Nenana River and north to include Wonder Lake.

1934
Charles S. Houston, Chychele Waterson and T. Graham Brown are the first to reach the summit of 17,400-foot Sultana, "Denali's Wife" (Mt. Foraker), the second-highest mountain in the park, and sixth highest in North America.

1939
Wonder Lake Ranger Station is built, and trails constructed to Horseshoe Lake and Triple Lakes. Visitors see the park's first sled dog demonstration. Wildlife biologist Adolf Murie begins his three-year study of the park's wolves that eventually becomes landmark research in predator-prey relationships, helping to destroy the myth that wolves are random, vicious killers.

1942
Prompted in part to defend Alaska from potential Japanese invasion, the 1,522-mile Alaska Highway is completed from Dawson Creek, British Columbia to Delta Junction, Alaska. Beginning in 1943, the Park Hotel serves as an Armed Forces R&R Center during World War II.

1947
Barbara Washburn becomes the first woman to reach the top of Denali (Mount McKinley).

1950
Sled dogs, off duty during the war years, return to the park kennels.

1956–1957
The Muldrow Glacier, the largest glacier on the north side of Denali (Mount McKinley), "surges" forward to within one mile of the park road between Eielson Visitor Center and Wonder Lake. By 1957, the Denali Highway is completed between Paxson and Cantwell, east of the park.

1967
Dave Johnston, Art Davidson and Ray Genet make the first winter ascent of Denali (Mount McKinley). While descending, they are trapped in a storm for six days, with a wind chill factor to −148° F. All three survive.

1971
The Alaska Native Claims Settlement Act (ANCSA) is passed, granting 44 million acres of land and one billion dollars to Alaska natives.

1972
The George Parks Highway, between Anchorage and Fairbanks, is completed. Park visitation jumps from 44,500 recreation visits to 88,615. A shuttle bus and reservations system are begun within the park, and Riley Creek Visitor Center opens. Fire consumes the Park Hotel.

1974
Mount McKinley National Park is designated a Biosphere Reserve, one of a network of protected samples of the world's major ecosystem types.

1976
A wildlife observation tower at Eielson Visitor Center is completed. On July 6, approximately 80 climbers, celebrating the American Bicentennial, reach the summit of Denali (Mount McKinley) in cloudless, windless conditions.

1980
With passage of the Alaska National Interest Lands Conservation Act (ANILCA)—the Louisiana Purchase of the American conservation movement—1.9 million-acre Mount McKinley National Park is enlarged to 6.0 million acres and renamed Denali National Park and Preserve; seven new national parks are created in Alaska.

1984
Japanese explorer Naomi Uemura makes the first solo winter ascent of Denali. Just after reaching the top, he disappears; his body has never been found.

1990
The Visitor Access Center is completed.

1992
The park celebrates its 75th anniversary.

DENALI'S MAJOR MAMMALS

MOOSE

(Bull, Cow, Calf)
Park population ~ 2,000 animals
Longevity: 17–20 years
Weight & size: Male ~ 1,000–1,600 lbs.
                Female ~ 800–1,200 lbs.
                Max. height at shoulder ~ 7.5 feet

Denali's moose migrate locally from river bottoms to willow patches, and may cover a 20–40 mile radius. Moose are herbivores; in spring they feed on sedges, grasses and pond weeds; in summer they may also eat willow, birch and aspen; winter diet includes twigs, bark and saplings. Moose first mate at 2–3 years, during September and October. After a 240-day gestation, one to three calves, weighing 28–35 lbs. at birth, are born in May and June. After five months, a calf may weigh over 300 lbs. Male moose antlers may reach 80 inches in width. Velvet is shed in August and September, the entire antler shed in November–December.

CARIBOU

(Bull, Cow, Calf, Herd)
Park population ~ 3,000 animals
Longevity: 11-12 years
Weight & size: Male ~ 359–400 lbs.
                Female ~ 175–225 lbs.
                Max. height at shoulder ~ 3.5–4 feet

Caribou herds migrate to and from calving areas—through the southeast region of Denali National Park and Preserve during summer months, moving toward the northwest region in winter. Herbivores, caribou feed on willow, grasses, dwarf birch and succulents in summer; winter diet includes lichens, moss and dried sedges. Caribou first mate at three years, during the month of October. After a 240-day gestation period, one calf (two are rare), weighing 10–15 lbs. at birth, is born in May or June. Caribou are the only member of the deer family in which both males and females have antlers. The antlers are shed each year: by males in December, and by pregnant females from April to June.

DALL SHEEP

(Ram, Ewe, Lamb, Band)
Park population ~ 2,500 animals
Longevity: 11-14 years
Weight & size: Female/Male ~ 125–200 lbs.
                Max. height at shoulder ~ 3–3.5 feet

Migrating between the Alaska Range and the Outer Range, these herbivores seek flowers, willows, sedges and grasses during summer, and mosses or lichens during winter months. Dall sheep first mate at three years, during November and December, although male and female sheep remain in separate bands until rut. Ewes give birth in May or June—every one to two years, depending on food supply—to one lamb (two are rare) after a 180-day gestation. As horns are never shed, horn rings can help determine a sheep's age—a male's horns reach full curl at 7–11 years. Wolves are the primary predator to Dall sheep bands.

GRIZZLY BEAR

(Boar, Sow, Cub)
Park population ~ 300 animals
Longevity: 16–20 years
Weight & size: Male ~ 300-500 lbs. (maximum 650 lbs.)
                Female ~ 200–400 lbs.
                Max. height at shoulder ~ 3.5 feet ~ 6–7 feet standing

Bears migrate locally throughout Denali National Park and Preserve; their home range varies. Bears are omnivores, eating a widely varied diet that includes 80–85% vegetation (roots, grasses, berries) and 15–20% meat (squirrels, moose or caribou calves). Bears reach sexual maturity at 6–10 years, depending on weight and age, and mate from May to July. They hibernate in winter, entering their solitary dens in October, and emerging in April. After a 180–day gestation, 1–4 cubs (twins are common) are born in their mother's den, weighing less than two pounds at birth. Sows live longer than boars, mating every three years or so, and have been known to adopt orphaned cubs.

GRAY WOLF

(Dog, Bitch, Pup, Pack)
Park population ~ 190 animals
Longevity: 9–12 years
Weight & size: Male ~ 85-115 lbs. ~ maximum 130 lbs.
                     Female ~ 75–105 lbs. ~ maximum 110 lbs.
                     Max. height at shoulder ~ 2.5 feet

Wolves migrate locally throughout the park, seeking
a varied carnivorous diet that includes rodents, hare,
beaver, birds, moose, caribou, sheep, bear, and carrion.
Each wolf pack may move over a 200–600 square mile
range, traveling up to fifty miles a day. Packs may be four
to eighteen wolves, or as many as thirty. Individual coat color varies from
black to white; gray shades are most common. Wolves begin mating at two
years, in February and March. After a 63-day gestation, two to ten pups (five
is average) are born, weighing one pound each at birth. Adult and juvenile
males as well as female wolves may assume the duties of supervising the pups
and teaching them to hunt.

RED FOX

(Dog, Vixen, Kit or Pup, Family)
Park population: no census known
Longevity: 10–14 years
Weight & size: Female/Male ~ 6–15 lbs.
                     Head and body ~ 22–25 inches long, plus 14–16 inch tail

Foxes are omnivores, moving locally throughout the park in search of
lemmings, squirrels, mice, insects, berries, eggs, birds, voles and a variety of
vegetation—they often bury food for future use. Foxes first mate at 1–2 years,
in February or March. After a 53-day gestation, vixens deliver four to ten kits
(four is average) weighing just four ounces at birth. Both parents care for the
young until the family unit breaks up in autumn. Silver, Cross, and Red Foxes
are all the same species—several color phases can occur in the same litter—
although all foxes have a white-tipped tail.

LYNX

(Male, Female, Kitten)
Park population: no census known
Longevity: 11-18 years
Weight & size: Female/Male ~ 11–35 lbs.
                     Approx. 3 feet long

The only cat to live in Alaska, lynx migrate locally through
the park, usually below treeline. These carnivores hunt
for hare, squirrel, rodents or ptarmigan, feeding on
carrion as well. Population numbers vary with the hare
population, peaking every 9–10 years. Lynx first mate at
one year, in January and February. Following a 62-day
gestation, 1–4 kittens (average is two) are born during March, April or May—
litter size varies with food supply. Lynx often hunt during evening hours. Their
large, broad feet serve as snowshoes.

HOARY MARMOT

Park population: no census known
Longevity: 5 years
Weight & size: Female/Male ~ 8–20 lbs. ~ maximum 30 lbs.
                     Body plus tail ~ 20–24 inches

Marmots burrow in rocky outcrops, where their whistled warnings can be
heard for up to two miles. These herbivores feed on grasses, flowering plants,
berries, roots, mosses and lichens; they are most active during daytime.
Marmots are true hibernators from September to April, arousing from a deep
sleep every two weeks to eat, defecate and urinate. They first mate at two years,
from March until May. After a 40-day gestation period, litters of two to six
young are born, weighing 1.5 ounces, during May and June.

*Information on Denali National Park and Preserve's history, flora and fauna is
condensed from National Park Service research documents and publications.*

MAMMAL CHECKLIST

INSECTIVORES

masked shrew	*Sorex cinereus*
dusky shrew	*Sorex monticolus*
tundra shrew	*Sorex tundrensis*
pygmy shrew	*Sorex hoyi*

BATS

little brown bat	*Myotis lucifugus*

PIKAS, HARES

collared pika	*Ochotona collaris*
snowshoe hare	*Lepus americanus*

RODENTS

hoary marmot	*Marmota caligata*
arctic ground squirrel	*Spermophilus parryii*
red squirrel	*Tamiasciurus hudsonicus*
northern flying squirrel	*Glaucomys sabrinus*
beaver	*Castor canadensis*
northern red-backed vole	*Clethrionomys rutilus*
meadow vole	*Microtus pennsylvanicus*
tundra vole	*Microtus oeconomus*
yellow-cheeked vole	*Microtus xanthognathus*
singing vole	*Microtus miurus*
muskrat	*Ondatra zibethicus*

brown lemming	*Lemmus trimucronatus*
northern bog lemming	*Mictomys borealis*
meadow jumping mouse	*Zapus hudsonius*
porcupine	*Erethizon dorsatum*

CARNIVORES

coyote	*Canis latrans*
wolf	*Canis lupus*
red fox	*Vulpes vulpes*
black bear	*Ursus americanus*
grizzly (brown) bear	*Ursus arctos*
marten	*Martes americana*
short-tailed weasel (ermine)	*Mustela erminea*
least weasel	*Mustela nivalis*
mink	*Mustela vison*
wolverine	*Gulo gulo*
river otter	*Lutra canadensis*
lynx	*Felis lynx*

HOOVED MAMMALS

moose	*Alces alces*
caribou	*Rangifer tarandus*
Dall sheep	*Ovis dalli*

Bird Checklist

Habitat ~ Lakes & Ponds

Common Loon
Red-throated Loon
Red-necked Grebe
Horned Grebe
Whistling Swan
Trumpeter Swan (rare)
Canada Goose (rare)
White-fronted Goose
Snow Goose (rare)
Mallard
Northern Pintail
Green-winged Teal
Blue-winged Teal
Northern Shoveler
American Wigeon
Canvasback (rare)
Redhead (rare)
Ring-necked Duck (rare)
Greater Scaup
Lesser Scaup
Common Goldeneye
Barrow's Goldeneye
Bufflehead
Oldsquaw
Harlequin Duck
White-winged Scoter
Surf Scoter
Black Scoter
Red-breasted Merganser (rare)
Bald Eagle (rare)
Sandhill Crane
Greater Yellowlegs (rare)
Lesser Yellowlegs
Solitary Sandpiper
Northern Phalarope
Common Snipe
Long-billed Dowitcher
Semipalmated Sandpiper (rare)
Western Sandpiper (rare)
Pectoral Sandpiper
Glaucous Gull
Bonaparte's Gull
Arctic Tern
Rusty Blackbird ◊
Savannah Sparrow

Habitat ~ Moist tundra

Northern Harrier
Swainson's Hawk (rare) □
Rough-legged Hawk (rare) □
Willow Ptarmigan
Whimbrel
Least Sandpiper □
Long-tailed Jaeger □
Snowy Owl
Short-eared owl

Habitat ~ Rocky Ridges

Say's Phoebe
Wheatear
Townsend's Solitaire

Habitat ~ Willow Thickets

Arctic Warbler
Yellow Warbler
Wilson's Warbler ≠
Red-winged Blackbird (occasional)

Habitat ~ River Bars

Semipalmated Plover
Spotted Sandpiper †
Wandering Tattler
Herring Gull (rare) †
Mew Gull †
Belted Kingfisher †
Alder Flycatcher ◊
Violet-green Swallow ‡
Bank Swallow
Barn Swallow (rare)
Cliff Swallow
Dipper

Habitat ~ Spruce Forest

Goshawk
Sharp-shinned Hawk
Red-tailed Hawk ‡
Merlin
American Kestrel
Spruce Grouse
Ruffed Grouse (occasional)
Rock Dove
Great-horned Owl
Hawk Owl
Great Gray Owl (rare)
Boreal Owl
Common Flicker
Hairy Woodpecker (rare)
Downy Woodpecker (rare)
Black-backed Woodpecker (rare)
Three-toed Woodpecker
Hammond's Flycatcher (rare)
Western Wood Pewee
Olive-sided Flycatcher
Tree Swallow
Gray Jay
Black-billed Magpie ◊
Common Raven
Back-capped Chickadee ◊
Gray-headed Chickadee (rare)
Boreal Chickadee
American Robin
Varied Thrush
Hermit Thrush
Swainson's Thrush
Gray-cheeked Thrush
Ruby-crowned Kinglet
Bohemian Waxwing
Northern Shrike §
Orange-crowned Warbler
Yellow-rumped Warbler
Blackpoll Warbler
Northern Waterthrush ◊
Pine Grosbeak
Hoary Redpoll
Common Redpoll
White-winged Crossbill
Dark-eyed Junco
Tree Sparrow §
White-crowned Sparrow ◊
Golden-crowned Sparrow ◊
Fox Sparrow ◊
Lincoln's Sparrow §

Habitat ~ Alpine tundra

Golden Eagle ‡
Gyrfalcon ‡
Rock Ptarmigan
White-tailed Ptarmigan ‡
American Golden Plover
Upland Sandpiper
Surfbird
Baird's Sandpiper
Horned Lark
Water Pipit
Gray-crowned Rosy Finch ‡
Lapland Longspur
Snow Bunting ‡

Accidental Species

Yellow-billed Loon
Arctic/Pacific Loon
Brant
Gadwall
European Wigeon
Killdeer
Ruddy Turnstone
Black Turnstone
Red Phalarope
Dunlin
Pomarine Jaeger
Sabine's Gull
Brown Creeper
Golden-crowned Kinglet
Starling
American Redstart
Brown-headed Cowbird
Pine Siskin

† also found at lakes, ponds
◊ also found in willow thickets
‡ also found on rocky ridges
§ also found on moist tundra
□ also found on alpine tundra
≠ also found in spruce forest

A complete bird checklist for Denali National Park & Preserve is available at Visitor Centers.

WILDFLOWERS

More than 600 species of trees, shrubs and herbs occur in Denali National Park and Preserve. The following is a list of 101 of the most commonly seen species of flowering plants; their common names, Latin names, habitat and approximate flowering times. The early bloomers are listed first, the late bloomers last.

HABITAT KEY

DT ~ dry tundra
RT ~ ridge tops, talus, scree
ST ~ shrub tundra
PM ~ pond margins
FO ~ forests, forest openings
GB ~ gravel bars
WT ~ wet tundra, wet meadows, snow flushes
DS ~ disturbed sites

COMMON NAME/ (LATIN NAME)	HABITAT/FLOWERING TIME			
	May	June	July	August
pasque flower Pulsatilla patens	FO————FO			
purple mountain saxifrage Saxifraga oppositifolia	GB—RT————————RT			
wooly lousewort Pedicularis lanata	RT————————DT			
blackish oxytrope Oxytropis nigrescens	RT ——————DT			
alpine azalea Loiseleuria procumbens	DT ———————DT			
windflower Anemone parviflora	DT ——————————DT			
Lapland rosebay Rhododendron lapponicum	DT————————DT			
narrow-petaled draba Draba stenopetala	RT——————————RT			
coltsfoot Petasites nivalis	~ ALL MOIST HABITATS ~			
arctic lupine Lupinus arcticus	FO–DT————————DT			
rock jasmine Androsace chamaejasme	RT——————————DT			
yellow anemone Anemone richardsonii	FO–WT——————WT			
bluebells Mertensia paniculata	FO—WT————————WT			
Parry's wallflower, parrya Parrya nudicaulis	FO—WT————————WT			
few-flowered corydalis Corydalis pauciflora	FO–WT —————WT			
shooting star Dodecatheon frigidum	WT———————————WT			
snow buttercup Ranunculus nivalis	WT——————————WT			

COMMON NAME/ (LATIN NAME)	HABITAT/FLOWERING TIME			
	May	June	July	August
Ross's avens Geum rossii	DT————————WT			
arctic bell heather Cassiope tetragona	DT————————DT			
alp lily Lloydia serotina	DT————————DT			
8-petaled Mountain avens Dryas octopetala	DT————————DT			
prickly saxifrage Saxifraga tricuspidata	DT/FO————————DT			
diapensia Diapensia lapponica	DT————————DT			
golden saxifrage Chrysosplenium wrightii	RT————————RT			
bunchberry, dogwood Cornus canadensis	FO————————FO			
sandwort Minuartia arctica	RT–DT————————RT			
tundra rose, shrubby cinquefoil Potentilla fruticosa	FO/ST————————DT			
mountain wormwood Artemisia tilesii	FO—DT————————DT			
yellow violet Viola biflora	DT————————WT			
dwarf forget-me-not Eritrichium chamissonis	RT————————RT			
forget-me-not Myosotis alpestris	DT————————DT			
king's crown Sedum rosea	RT/DT————————WT			
primrose Primula eximia	WT————WT			
alpine draba Draba alpina	RT————————RT			
bistort, pink plume Polygonum bistorta	DT—WT————————WT			
capitate lousewort Pedicularis capitata	DT————————DT			
blueberry Vaccinium uglinosum	DT/FO/WT–WT			
mountain sorrel Oxyria digyna	DT/FO/WT————DT			
Alaska poppy Papaver alaskanum	RT/GB————————RT/GB			
white dryas Dryas integrifolia	DT—GB——DT			
alpine milk vetch, mountain locoweed Astragalus alpinus	DS/GB——————DS/GB			
Scamman's spring beauty Claytonia scammaniana	RT————RT			
death camas Zygadenus elegans	DT/FO————————DT/FO			
sourdock, arctic dock Rumex arcticus	DT–WT————DT			
Alaska spring beauty Claytonia sarmentosa	DT/WT————————DT			
purplish bittercress Cardamine pupurea	DT————RT——WT			
oxytrope Oxytropis viscida	GB/DT————GB/DT			
wild sweet pea, bear root Hedysarum alpinum	DT/GB/FO——————DT/GB/FO			
wild celery Angelica lucida	DT————————WT			
cow parsnip Heracleum lanatum	WT————————WT			

COMMON NAME/ (LATIN NAME)	HABITAT/FLOWERING TIME
	May · June · July · August
shy maiden *Moneses uniflora*	FO————FO
bog rosemary *Andromeda polifolia*	WT/PM—————WT
starflower *Trientalis europaea*	FO—————WT
moss campion *Silene acaulis*	RT/DT———RT
brook saxifrage *Saxifraga nelsoniana*	DT–WT———DT
mouse-eared chickweed	DT/WT———RT
Cerastium beeringianum	
merckia *wilhelmsia physodes*	FO————FO
marsh marigold *Caltha palustris*	WT/PM——WT/PM
Macoun's poppy *Papaver macounii*	RT/GB————RT/GB
cuckoo flower *Cardamine pratensis*	WT/FO/PM–WT/FO/PM
round-leaved sundew *Drosera rotundifolia*	WT———PM
red-stemmed saxifrage *Saxifraga lyallii*	WT———WT
wild rose *Rosa acicularis*	DT/FO————DT
wild geranium, cranesbill	DT——WT——DT
Geranium erianthum	
Alaska violet *Viola langsdorfii*	DT–WT———DT
tall fireweed *Epilobium angustifolium*	DS—————DS
dwarf fireweed *Epilobium latifolium*	DT—GB—RT——GB
pink pyrola, wintergreen *Pyrola asariflora*	FO————FO
one-sided pyrola, one-sided wintergreen	FO————FO
Pyrola secunda	
pixie eyes, wedge-leaved primrose	DT——DT
Primula cuneifolia	
weaselsnout *Lagotis glauca*	WT———WT
Sudeten lousewort *Pedicularis sudetica*	FO/GB——FO/GB
Oeder's lousewort *Pedicularis oederi*	WT–DT———DT
twin flower *Linnaea borealis*	FO————FO
goldenrod *Solidago multiradiata*	FO–DT————DT
Lessing's arnica *Arnica lessingii*	DT————DT
frigid arnica *Arnica frigida*	RT————DT
black-tipped groundsel *Senecio lugens*	FO–DT———DT
dwarf hawk's beard *Crepis nana*	GB——DS———GB
Siberian aster *Aster sibiricus*	FO–DT————FO
monkshood *Aconitum delphinifolium*	DT–WT/FO———WT
bearflower, Alaska boykinia	DT/WT——WT
Boykinia richardsonii	
spotted saxifrage *Saxifraga bronchialis*	RT—————RT

COMMON NAME/ (LATIN NAME)	HABITAT/FLOWERING TIME
	May · June · July · August
grass of parnassus *Parnassia palustris*	~ ALL HABITATS EXCEPT RT ~
sibbaldia *Sibbaldia procumbens*	DT———WT
Sitka burnet *Sanguisorba officinalis*	DT———WT
four-parted gentian *Gentiana propinqua*	DT–FO————WT
tall Jacob's ladder	FO–WT————WT
Polemonium acutiflorum	
elegant paintbrush *Castilleja elegans*	DT————DT
Labrador lousewort	FO————FO
Pedicularis labradorica	
Saussurea *Saussurea angustifolia*	DT–WT————WT
arctic senecio *Senecio atropurpureus*	RT——RT/DT
frog orchis *Coeloglossom viride*	DT——DT
dwarf larkspur *Delphinium chamissonis*	RT——RT
larkspur *Delphinium glaucum*	DT/WT/FO——WT
yellow marsh saxifrage, bog saxifrage	WT————WT
Saxifraga hirculus	
wild heliotrope *Valeriana capitata*	WT/FO———FO
mountain harebell *Campanula lasiocarpa*	DT————DT
whitish gentian *Gentiana algida*	DT————DT
pale paintbrush *Castilleja caudata*	FO————FO
northern bedstraw *Galium boreale*	WT————WT